Luck of the Irish?
More Like Mom's Magic in Éire!

Luck of the Irish?
More Like Mom's Magic in Éire!

Hey there! So, let's talk about Ireland, or as the Irish call it, Éire (it's pronounced like "air-uh," by the way). Cool name, right? Well, it's not just any name. Ireland and Éire actually come from this old-school Irish word "Ériu." Now, get this: Ériu isn't just any word; it's the name of a super important goddess in Irish mythology. She's not your average goddess, though; she's the goddess of sovereignty. Yep, that means she's basically the boss lady of the land. And guess what? People have been talking about her since way back in the ninth century. So next time you hear "Ireland" or "Éire," remember, you're basically name-dropping a goddess. How cool is that?]

# Chapter 1
# My Crazy Little Life

So here's the deal: living in a hole, no money, boring work. Sounds like a total bummer, right? But hang in there, because I promise you, it's not all doom and gloom. I've got some funny bits to share, some facepalm moments, and yeah, a bit of that 'how the heck did I get here?' kind of vibe.

Let's kick off with a bit of family wisdom. My dad, bless his heart, was all about keeping it local when it came to love. 'Don't go marrying someone from a whole different world,' he'd say, 'It's just asking for trouble.' Well, guess what? His daughters didn't really take that to heart. My sis and I, we're rocking the single mom life in Europe, miles away from Latin American roots. But hey, that's a story for another day.

Now, let me paint you a picture of my place in Budapest. Calling it a 'one-bedroom' is super generous. It's more like a 'one-room' where you do everything. And the kitchen? Oh, it's a laugh. Imagine trying to whip up a meal in a space so tiny you'd struggle to swing a cat. It's got this sad little counter that's just a plank of wood, and don't even get me started on the rickety stove.

My so-called bedroom? It's a loft. And by loft, I mean a tiny space where you can barely sit up without bumping your head. Each morning is like playing a game of 'will I or won't I smack my head today?' Spoiler: I usually do.

Living here's like being in a comedy show where the joke's mostly on me. But it's home. And it's where I've had to get creative, like turning a cramped space into somewhere me and my son can actually live. We've got boxes for clothes, a bed that's also a couch, and a window where we can spy on the world outside without anyone noticing.

Back when I was a kid, life was all about big open spaces, playing with my huge dog, and having adventures up in the mountains. Now, it's about navigating a tiny apartment and a job that's so boring it could win awards. Seriously, I work from home sometimes, and it's like, 'Yay, an email! Something to do!'

Then there's the school run, a whole adventure on its own. My boy's school isn't far, but crossing the road is like a mini survival challenge, dodging cars that seem to think stopping is optional.

So, yeah, it's a bit of a madhouse. But it's our madhouse. And I'm here to share all the nutty, weird, and downright hilarious stuff that happens. Because if you can't laugh at the craziness of life, what can you do, right? Welcome to the chaos—I hope you're ready for some laughs!

# Chapter 2
# The Daily Grind and Dreams of Escape

Welcome back to my rollercoaster of a life, where every day is a new adventure in 'how will we make it through this time?' The title of this chapter could well be 'What on Earth Are We Going to Eat?' Yep, that's a frequent brain teaser in my world.

Here's the deal: making ends meet on a tight budget is like playing a game where the rules keep changing. Rent, bills, food, and let's not forget, Adam's outgrowing his shoes faster than I can say 'not again.' We're in Budapest, trying to live our best lives, but sometimes it feels more like survival mode.

So there I am, at work, daydreaming about a better life in Spain. 'Why Spain?' you might ask. Well, I've got a soft spot for it, having spent my childhood in Madrid. Plus, I figured speaking Spanish could open more doors than Hungarian—no offense to Hungary, it's just, you know, practical thinking.

My buddy Esmeralda's at my side while I'm spamming companies with my CV, hoping for a miracle. But, spoiler alert, it's not going as planned. Most companies ghost me the moment they find out I'm not local. Talk about a bummer.

Meanwhile, back at the ranch, Adam's school life is another story. His Hungarian's not top-notch, and his teacher's suggesting he repeats a grade. Yeah, like that's going to happen. We're not sticking around that long, lady!

And oh, let's chat about Adam's dad, Diego. He's more like a whirlwind that pops in, causes chaos, and disappears. The guy's idea of sharing is snatching the biggest chunk of chocolate from his own kid. Not cool, Diego, not cool. So, we decided it's bye-bye, Diego time. Adam's way happier without the drama.

But life loves to throw curveballs, right? Just when I thought things couldn't get crazier, my landlord wants to hike up the rent. For this tiny box of an apartment? Seriously? I'm all for living in a nice area, but not when it means going broke.

Speaking of the area, let's touch on a sensitive topic. Budapest has its share of problems, like any city. My grandma had a scary encounter with some folks trying to scam her. It's tough, especially when you're trying to stay positive and not stereotype, but experiences like these can really shake you up.

So, there you have it, chapter two of my not-so-boring life. It's a mix of job hunting, school drama, dodging rent hikes, and keeping the past, well, in the past. But hey, we're still here, still kicking, and who knows what tomorrow will bring? Stay tuned, because this single mom's journey is anything but predictable.

# Chapter 3
# New Beginnings and Goodbyes

Alright, folks, strap in for chapter three, where things start looking up (kinda). Life at the old job threw me a curveball—a chance to step up as a team leader. Sounds cool, right? But here's the kicker: the fancy title wouldn't really fatten up my wallet. And let's be real, a title doesn't feed you or pay the rent.

Just when I was mulling over this 'big opportunity,' along came a game-changer. I landed a gig at Diageo as a master data specialist. Sounds fancy, huh? The best part? It paid better and was a hop, skip, and a tram ride away from Adam's school. No more epic commutes for this mama!

Breaking the news to my boss wasn't easy. He was all sad puppy eyes, saying they had big plans for me. But hey, a mom's gotta do what a mom's gotta do, right? I thanked him for everything, waved goodbye to my work pals and Esmeralda, and set off for Diageo.

Let me tell you, Diageo was a breath of fresh air compared to the snooze fest at IBM. I was buzzing, feeling like I was finally getting somewhere. But, plot twist—I already had my sights set on another country. Yeah, I'm restless like that.

Meanwhile, back at IBM, Esmeralda stepped into my could-have-been shoes as team leader. She's killing it and has since moved on to bigger things in banking. We don't get to hang as much, but she's still my ride-or-die.

So, there you have it—chapter three is all about new starts, tough goodbyes, and keeping the dream alive. Onward and upward, right?

# Chapter 4
# Operation Move-Out and Mom's Place Mayhem

Alrighty, welcome to Chapter 4, where summer's in full swing, and I'm cooking up a new plan. Since the whole 'find a job abroad' mission was moving slower than a snail on vacation, I decided it was time to ditch the grumpy landlord and our cramped apartment.

So, the grand scheme? Crash at my mom's for a bit. And when I say 'a bit,' I mean three months. Oh, and I ghosted the landlord. Yep, just packed up and left. He was Mr. Nasty Email, preferring to harass me from a safe distance rather than confront me face to face. Talk about a coward, right?

The moving day was like a scene from a sitcom. My friend rocked up in her car, but could we fit all our stuff in one go? Of course not. That'd be too easy. She had to dash off, promising to return for the second load, leaving me biting my nails, worrying the landlord might pop by.

And let me tell you about the magic of the word 'free' in Hungary. I left some plants outside with a 'free to a good home' sign, and bam, they vanished faster than ice cream on a hot day. In Hungary, if it's free, it's irresistible. Anyway, we made a sneaky exit, keys left in the letterbox, and poof, we were gone before Mr. Landlord knew what hit him.

I'll admit, bailing on the rental like a ninja wasn't my proudest moment, but the guy was a piece of work. Always after more money, never showing me the bills. I swear he was charging me for his own utilities. So, leaving behind the convertible bed and the electric oven (which, by the way, was a godsend since the apartment had none) felt like a fair trade.

Now, moving in with Mom should've been smooth sailing, right? Wrong. My sister threw a fit. She acted like she owned the place because she crashed there during her pregnancy. Sure, she had her drama, but come on, it's our mom's place, not her personal kingdom.

Despite her grumbling, I moved in, paying my share of the bills (more than I can say for her). It was a bit of a circus, but hey, that's family for you. So there we were, bunking with Mom, navigating sibling squabbles, and plotting our next move. Stay tuned, because the adventure's just getting started.

# Chapter 5
# The Great Spanish Adventure

Chapter five, here we go! Fasten your seatbelts, 'cause we're off to Spain! After saving up for three months, Adam and I were ready to trade Budapest's charm for Spain's sunny shores. Barcelona was our dream, but after some hardcore Googling, I realized my wallet had other plans. So, Torremolinos in Málaga County became our new target—way cheaper and supposedly job-friendly. Spoiler alert: it wasn't as easy as I thought.

We met Alejandro, a cool Mexican dude living in Torremolinos with his Russian wife and their kiddo. He hooked us up with a temporary crash pad and suggested job hunting in Málaga might be better. Before we knew it, Adam was enrolled in a school there, and off we flew, waving goodbye to Grandma at the airport.

Our arrival was straight out of a travel-gone-wrong show. Struggling with hefty suitcases, deciphering train stops with a busted info panel, and trudging through the streets of Torremolinos—it was an Olympic sport, and Adam was about to lose it.

Alejandro's place was cozy, and their hospitality was a lifesaver. Ever heard of couch surfing? That's how we met Alejandro. It's all about sharing your space for free, meeting folks from around the globe, and snagging cultural karma points for when you're the traveler.

Fast forward to school runs in Málaga, and me burning through my savings on train tickets while job hunting in posh malls with snail-paced Wi-Fi. Picture me, a desperate mom squatting in fancy shops, scouting for cheap rentals and work online.

Turns out, finding a place in Málaga was a bust. So, back to Torremolinos we went, where the vibe was more our style—chill and welcoming. Just when we started feeling at home, Alejandro got antsy and hinted we should fly back to Budapest. Dude, it's been a week and a half, give us a break!

But hey, luck was on our side. We found a sweet one-bedroom apartment by the beach, and Adam got his own room for the first time. Our new home was cozy, except for the noisy neighbor who seemed to love shouting at his wife at all hours—welcome to Spain, right?

Now, about getting a job. Spain's bureaucracy is like a crazy maze. No job without a social security number, but no number without a job. Eventually, a UK company in Málaga threw me a lifeline, and I snagged that precious social security number.

The new gig? Let's just say it was... interesting. It involved cold-calling and pushing services on folks. Not my cup of tea. After a day of listening to sales spiels and feeling the commission-pressure cooker, I bailed. Yep, just texted the boss, 'Adios!' and kept my job hunt alive.

So there you have it—Chapter 5 is all about diving into the unknown, juggling the joys of

Spanish bureaucracy, and learning that sometimes, you've got to trust your gut and say 'nope' to a job that just doesn't fit. Onward to the next adventure!

# Chapter 6
# Seaside Struggles and Vending Machine Surprises

Here we are in chapter six, where the sunny shores of Torremolinos become our new backdrop. There's something magical about living by the sea, a dream I've always had, now a reality. It's like the world's worries just drift away with the waves.

Back in Budapest, the Danube was my escape, chilling with my Irish Setter (oh, the irony of 'Irish' didn't hit me until now!). Now, it's the Mediterranean's turn to be my serene companion while Adam's at school.

Without internet at home, the local library became our new hangout. It's where Adam could dive into tablet adventures, and I could continue the relentless job hunt. We even made a new friend, Aisha, who shared some local wisdom, like ditching the pricey train for a more budget-friendly bus. Gotta love those insider tips!

As Christmas neared, I tried to keep the magic alive for Adam, blending Hungarian traditions with Spain's 'Reyes Magos.' Because, let's be honest, who doesn't want to wake up to a pile of gifts in January?

But reality was tough. Job hunting was a bust. Even a potential gig with a decent salary fell through because, apparently, I'm not cut out for debt collection. Who knew?

Torremolinos had its quirks. I discovered a world of vending machines selling everything from snacks to, believe it or not, sex toys. Yep, you read that right. And let's not forget the Chinese shops – those places are like Aladdin's caves of randomness where you can find literally anything.

Despite the oddities and charms of our new home, making ends meet was a struggle. I even tried selling handmade crochet baskets, but no luck there. Our financial lifeline became charity support and a bit of help from my mom and Esmeralda. Rent was overdue, and Christmas was looming. How was I going to explain to Adam that Santa and the 'Reyes Magos' might skip our house this year?

Life in Torremolinos was a mix of beachside bliss and harsh realities. Between vending machine discoveries and the kindness of strangers, we were riding the rollercoaster of expat life, trying to find our footing in this vibrant, quirky town. On to the next chapter, where hopefully, things start looking up!

# Chapter 7
# The Not-So-Merry Pre-Christmas Saga

Alrighty, chapter seven, and boy, do I have a story for you! It's mid-December, and the job hunt's going as well as a snowball fight in the Sahara. To add to the festive spirit, our landlord's on the warpath, threatening to trek from Sevilla to Torremolinos just to kick us out. Talk about holiday cheer, huh?

Now, enter stage left: Adam's grandma, a visitor from our past, popping over from Argentina via Madrid, where she was visiting her other grandkid. Our families are like a global soap opera—she's got sons in Madrid playing padel (it's like tennis but quirkier), and there's a sprinkle of Basque, German, Polish, Slovakian, Argentinean, and possibly a dash of Jewish in our genetic cocktail. Confused? Imagine how our family reunions must look!

So, Grandma Mirta decides to drop in. Last time we met, she seemed sweet, but oh, how appearances can deceive! She swoops into our life, cranking up the electricity use (not like I'm counting pennies or anything), and then—get this—she balks at buying Adam a €6 toy car because it's 'too expensive.' Yet, she's contemplating an €80 suit for her cousin. Priorities, right?

She drags me around Torremolinos, eyeing fridge magnets that scream 'world's best granddaughter' and 'world's best dad,' but apparently, the 'world's best grandson' section was missing. And there I was, just 'the mother,' watching her skip the magnet for Adam. I mean, if you're not going to spoil your grandson, why bother visiting?

In the end, she jetted off without leaving a dime, not even a little something for Adam. So, I made an executive decision—Grandma Mirta's out of our lives. No more faux niceties, no more energy vampires in our tiny Torremolinos abode. We're trimming down our Christmas list, and it feels surprisingly liberating!

So, that's the lowdown on our pre-Christmas shenanigans. Stay tuned for what's next, because with our family, it's always a wild ride!

# Chapter 8
# Fishy Business and Holiday Hustles

Alright, dive into Chapter 8, where my life takes a turn for the, well, aquatic. Just when the landlord's threat level hit 'Santa's naughty list,' I stumble upon a job opening at a fish spa. Yes, you heard right—a place where tiny fish nibble at your feet. Tourists can't get enough of it, and there I was, smack in the middle of this fishy frenzy.

The shop was owned by a Brit who was apparently playing hide and seek with debt collectors back in Torremolinos. The place was a hodgepodge of characters, including a

Colombian tattoo artist who was literally making his mark on the Costa del Sol crowd. This job was an odd mix of dull and bizarre. Imagine spending your days watching fish perform pedicures. My colleague, Olivia, had her own share of chaos, involving hash, hallucinogens, and a dog with a penchant for getting into things it shouldn't. Just another day in paradise, right?

Torremolinos turned out to be the town where every day is a Pride parade. The place was buzzing with energy, and not just from the LGBTQ-friendly vibes. I even got a bizarre proposal from a local Casanova who thought I'd jump at the chance to be his live-in Cinderella. No thanks, buddy!

Adam hung out with me at the spa in the afternoons, turning our workplace into a makeshift family hub. We had to get creative with our Wi-Fi mooching, thanks to the owner's aversion to bill-paying. Even the fish had a blackout scare, but crisis was averted, keeping our scaly staff members in business.

Life in Spain really makes you a night owl. With Adam's bedtime rivaling mine for lateness, we were living on a distinctly Spanish schedule, complete with late dinners and even later bedtimes.

Then came the Christmas conundrum. Adam, bless his heart, set his sights on a Nintendo Switch. With my fish spa salary? Dream on! I managed to get him a Nintendo 2DS XL instead, hoping he wouldn't notice the difference. But kids are smart, aren't they? He figured Santa got a bit mixed up but remained hopeful the Reyes Magos would correct the error. Oh, the innocence!

Eventually, I had to spill the beans about Santa and the Reyes Magos. It was a tough pill for Adam to swallow, but he took it like a champ, appreciating the years of magical Christmases we'd managed to create.

Torremolinos had its quirks, from candy-throwing Kings in parades to adults elbowing kids for sweets (yep, that's a thing). Despite the challenges, we were making the most of our seaside saga, one fishy foot spa and festive faux pas at a time.

# Chapter 9
# Embroidery and Harbor Life

Jump into Chapter 9, where life's about to get a stitch more interesting! Still at the fish spa in February, trying to juggle pennies to keep the landlord off my back. Paying rent in bits and pieces isn't ideal, but hey, it's better than an eviction notice, right?

Then, Antonio, the guy who helps manage the landlord's properties, turns out to be a real gem. He even drops off some hand-me-downs for Adam and me. Talk about a wardrobe refresh! As a token of gratitude, I whip up one of my crochet baskets for him and throw in a bottle of wine. Choosing wine in a Spanish grocery store when you're alcohol intolerant is no small feat, let me tell you!

But change is in the air. My stint at the spa is wrapping up, and it's time to find something new. Enter Benalmádena, the next chapter in our Spanish saga. It's a stone's throw from Torremolinos but feels worlds apart. I land a job at a harbor shop, embroidering names on baby items. A bit more upscale than fish pedicures, wouldn't you say?

The harbor's a bustling spot, brimming with tourists, boats, and a sense of community. I'm selling personalized baby gear, working alongside a mix of Bulgarians, Spaniards, and even a Chilean. It's a creative gig, deciding which fonts make baby blankets look chic and which ones are a no-go.

Viktor, my new boss, is a breath of fresh air compared to the debt-dodging owner of the fish spa. The harbor feels like a little village where everyone knows your name, from the sightseeing boat guys to the restaurant staff nearby.

But it's not all smooth sailing. When rain hits —which is rare but dramatic in Torremolinos —we scramble to protect the embroidery machine and merchandise. And getting Adam to school on rainy mornings? It's an exercise in creativity, navigating Spanish school gate protocols and a sea of 'rain, rain, rain...' excuses in the late sign-in book.

Life in Benalmádena's harbor is a blend of work and play. I even snag a free boat ride just for being a harbor 'local.' And next door, there's a quirky photo tent where you can get snapped in swing era getup. It's a colorful, lively place, and for the first time in a while, I'm not just going through the motions—I'm actually enjoying myself.

To top it off, I've upgraded my commute with a good old-fashioned scooter. No, not one of those fancy electric ones—a kick scooter. It's me, zipping along the beachfront, heading to a job that's as refreshing as the Mediterranean breeze.

So there you have it, Chapter 9's all about new beginnings, community vibes, and finding joy in the unexpected. From fish nibbling at toes to stitching names on tiny towels, it's just another chapter in our ever-surprising Spanish adventure!

# Chapter 10
# Budgie Adventures and Hilltop Hikes

Welcome to Chapter 10, where our lives take a chirpy turn! Living next to the beach in Torremolinos sounds like a dream, right? Well, add a steep hill to the mix, the kind you tackle every day to get Adam to school, and you've got yourself a daily workout that would make a mountain goat proud.

On our daily ascent, we'd pass this pet shop, a cacophony of budgies and parrots serenading the street. Around here, you don't just hear the caged birds; the town's got its own wild soundtrack thanks to the green Monk parakeets that are local celebs, nesting in palm trees and living the high life.

Adam had been bugging me for a dog, but our apartment was more sardine can than sprawling estate, so we compromised. Enter Carmen, the not-so-ordinary, greenish-yellow budgie who stole our hearts in the pet shop. She was affordable, adorable, and just the right size for our cozy home. Soon, feeling that Carmen needed company, we introduced Blue, Grey, and Luna into the mix, turning our place into a mini bird sanctuary.

Our apartment was alive with the sound of budgie banter, with the foursome ruling the roost from their curtain rod throne. It was like having a piece of the wild indoors, minus the palm trees.

But then, drama struck. Carmen, our feathery pioneer, was found on the floor one night, looking more like a fluffy ball than a bird. Despite my all-night cuddle session, trying to nurse her back to health, we woke up to find her gone, leaving us with just a bundle of feathers and heavy hearts. Adam was devastated. It was his first pet loss, a rite of passage that hit him hard.

Not long after, Luna showed similar symptoms. This time, we weren't taking any chances. The vet diagnosed a common pet shop bird ailment—a bacterial gut infection. Armed with medicine and a fishing net (yep, you read that right), we embarked on a bird-catching, medicine-distributing mission that would make any wildlife show proud. Thankfully, Luna bounced back, sparing us and the budgie squad further heartache.

So there we were, a little family in Torre-molinos, learning life lessons from a quartet of budgies. Between hill climbs, vet visits, and unexpected goodbyes, we were dis-covering that even in the smallest creatures, there are big stories to be told.

# Chapter 11
# A Twist of Fate and Benalmádena Bliss

Here we are in Chapter 11, where our little family's journey takes an uplifting turn. It's April, and suddenly, life's looking a bit sunnier. After years of waiting, we finally sell a problematic property my dad left behind. Imagine a house with no permits and a load of legal hiccups. Yep, that was our little goldmine, stubbornly refusing to be sold until now. But as luck would have it, the place turns trendy, and just like that, we're in the money!

Now, I've heard folks say, 'Money doesn't buy happiness.' Well, I'm not entirely convinced because suddenly, doors began to open, literally. We'd been eyeing Benalmádena, a town that stole my heart at first sight, and now, thanks to our newfound fortune, we could actually consider moving there.

Finding a rental wasn't a walk in the park, though. Mention you're selling baby clothes down at the harbor, and suddenly, apartments become 'unavailable.' But then, a colleague shares the magic trick: offer to pay six months' rent upfront. Bingo! The previously 'unavailable' apartment suddenly reappears on the market.

So, we move into this fantastic place in Benalmádena, a stone's throw from the harbor and the beach. The building's got pools, a concierge, and a charming old-school vibe, complete with vintage phones that look like they belong in a museum.

Adam transitions to a new school, and it's a whole different ball game. No more endless homework sessions post-fish spa work. We even transform the living room wall into an educational exhibit, plastering it with river maps and multiplication tables.

Life in our new abode is like a constant vacation. Pools, parks, and even a zoo camp where Adam gets up close with dolphins and sea lions. And let's not forget about our adventures in the local parks and neighboring towns, where animals seem just as much a part of the community as the people.

Then there's Laura, Adam's new babysitter and possibly the coolest makeup artist slash fun companion around. She transforms Adam into the most terrifying Jeff the Killer for Halloween, wins the award for 'Best Homemade Costume' in our book, and becomes a cherished part of our lives.

In the midst of this newfound happiness, our balcony becomes a sanctuary for our budgie family, now thriving and expanding. Life's full of little surprises, like a new feathered friend who just decides to join the party.

Working late shifts at the harbor, I'm grateful for Laura, who ensures Adam's evenings are filled with fun and creativity. From pool days to fairs, she's not just a sitter; she's a gateway to new experiences for Adam.

So, Chapter 11 is all about change, new beginnings, and the joys that come with a bit of financial freedom. From a troublesome property sale to tranquil days in Benalmádena, it's a reminder that sometimes, just sometimes, money can pave the way to a slice of happiness.

# Chapter 12
# The Australian Dream Takes a Detour to Cork

Welcome to Chapter 12, where life throws a curveball, and our plans take a scenic route! It's April, and fortune smiles on us with a surprise inheritance from Dad's property – a plot that's been more drama than real estate for the last 12 years. Who knew hidden faults and legal tangles could finally turn into a golden ticket?

With this windfall, I'm daydreaming about business ventures in Benalmádena, but watching my boss Viktor and the neighboring Bulgarian entrepreneur Gigi stress over tourist footfall kills the vibe. Business, as it turns out, is synonymous with stress, no matter the sunny setting.

Then there's the boat idea – dolphin tours in Puerto Marina, how picturesque! Yet Viktor, the voice of experience, pops that bubble faster than you can say 'captain.' Turns out, the harbor's more Game of Thrones than Flipper with its turf wars and overheads.

Australia beckons in my dreams, the land of kangaroos, koalas, and, apparently, my zen future. I've got the gardening creds, a plan to polish my English in Perth, and a vision of Adam and me embracing the Aussie life. Yet reality check – Aussie schools aren't cheap, and the visa folks want a solid reason why we'd ever leave Down Under. Cue existential crisis about money, future plans, and whether my landscape gardening aspirations stand a chance against Aussie job market realities.

As Benalmádena's tourist tide ebbs, I'm hitting the books behind my stand, questioning life choices and missing the intellectual banter of my IBM days. Costa del Sol's charm is undeniable, but I'm craving a challenge, something to sink my brain into beyond the realm of baby bibs and tourist trinkets.

Enter Ireland, land of the chatty, cheerful folk who make pride contagious. Cork calls my name, not just because of a job ad from Apple that painted it as an emerald Eden but because a former IBM colleague promised it's awesome (though I take that with a pinch of Hungarian skepticism). Ireland, where people are said to be the Spanish of the north –

friendly, welcoming, and maybe just the place to find our happy ever after.

So, I pivot from Aussie beaches to Irish greens, setting sights on Cork with a new-found mission: to crack into cybersecurity. It's a leap from landscape gardening in Perth, but who says you can't reinvent yourself? Plus, the allure of understanding what makes the Irish so darn joyful is too tempting to resist.

I announce our grand plan: Cork, here we come, ready to embrace cybersecurity and all the Irish charm we can handle. It's a bold move, a world away from my original Down Under dream, but sometimes, life's detours lead to the most exciting destinations. So, buckle up – we're off to Ireland, chasing dreams, and maybe a leprechaun or two along the way.

# Chapter 13
# The Cork Adventure Begins

Welcome to Chapter 13, where our Spanish saga takes a turn toward the Irish charm! As the harbor job wrapped up, November found me and Adam gearing up for a rental hunt in Cork, armed with optimism and a dash of my usual luck.

Landing in Cork, I instantly felt like I'd come home. We checked into a hostel, aiming for budget-friendly digs, but ended up in a private room (bunk beds and all!) because the kind-hearted receptionist couldn't bear to mix Adam with potentially rowdy roomies. There we were, me hunting for rentals on my phone while Adam battled virtual foes on his Nintendo.

The rental scene in Cork was a shocker – prices were sky-high compared to our cozy Benalmádena setup. I dived into Facebook groups, battling a sea of opportunists and scammers, trying to find us a new nest. One lady even tried to lure me into paying upfront for a phantom apartment! Nice try, but no dice.

As our week was winding down, I was torn between extending our hunt or heading back to Spain for one last Spanish Christmas and a final Reyes Magos celebration. But fate, as always, had a plan. A message pinged in – a Spanish lady with a room and a heart of gold, offering us a place in her multicultural household. No money upfront, just pure trust. And just like that, Cork went from a maybe to a definitely in our books.

We'd be coming back in January, stepping into 2019 with a new chapter in Cork, a city where rentals are rarer than four-leaf clovers. Luck, my old friend, seemed to stick by my side, making sure our Irish story started on a high note.

So there we were, ready to swap palm trees for shamrocks, pools for pubs, and embark on an adventure in a land known for its warmth (in spirit, if not always in weather). Cork, get ready, because here we come, ready to soak in the Irish way of life and maybe, just maybe, find that elusive pot of gold at the end of the rainbow (or at least a decent cup of tea)."

# Chapter 14
# A Sunny Christmas and New Year's in Benalmádena.

Chapter 14 unfolds as we soak up the festive season in sunny Benalmádena, swapping snowflakes for sunshine. There's something surreal about Christmas trees basking in 26°C heat while we stroll along the beach, a far cry from the chilly Christmases back in Hungary, where the cold bites through layers of winter gear.

Our holiday season was a blend of traditional and tropical. Amid daily beach walks, we reveled in the local customs. Viktor, my ex-boss, roped us into a merry dinner with summer colleagues, infusing warmth into the winter air. Then, there was the New Year's celebration with Paula and Sani, our friends from the apartment saga, where we embraced the Spanish grape-eating tradition at midnight—popping grapes to the chime of the clock, hoping for good fortune in the coming year.

Comparing traditions, I realized how diverse Christmas can be. In Hungary, December starts with boots filled with treats from Saint Nicholas—if you're good, that is. Then, baby Jesus sneaks in on Christmas Eve, leaving presents under the tree, a magical notion I cherished as a kid, even trying to track his snowy footprints once. And while Hungary parties hard on New Year's Eve, Spain has its unique grape tradition, uniting families in a quirky countdown to luck.

Easter in Hungary has its charm too, with men reciting poems and dousing women with cologne in exchange for decorated eggs—though nowadays, chocolate and bunnies are more the rage. And let's not forget Hungary's somber Independence Day, where classical tunes set a melancholic backdrop to dazzling fireworks—a mix of celebration and reflection.

Back in Benalmádena, our Spanish Christmas was a blend of new experiences and heartfelt goodbyes as we prepared for our upcoming adventure in Cork. Amid the festive joy, there was an undercurrent of anticipation for the unknown awaiting us in Ireland. So, with one last Spanish Christmas under our belt, we were ready to leap into the next chapter, chasing new traditions and creating more

memories in a land famous for its emeralds
and, hopefully, a little less for its rain.

# Chapter 15
# The Cork Chronicles

Welcome to Chapter 15, where we dive into our new life in Cork, juggling suitcases, hunting for rentals, and adapting to our Irish adventure. Our journey kicks off with the enchanting 'Reyes Magos' parade, a sweet farewell filled with candies and goodbyes, setting the stage for our departure from sunny Benalmádena.

January 9th rolls around, and there we are at Málaga airport, wrestling with eight suitcases like a pair of nomads. The security check becomes a mini-epic of unpacking and repacking, a test of patience and packing skills. Our trek to the gate is a saga on its own, complete with a lost ticket drama that has us racing against time, only to discover that, in the end, a simple reprint at the gate could have saved us all the fuss.

Landing in Cork, the reality of our move hits us. We're in Pedro and Mayte's world now, a Spanish-Irish household fusion with its quirks and challenges. Their house, brimming with character (and a few repair needs), becomes our new base. Privacy is scarce, the kitchen's always bustling, and the garden's not quite the serene retreat one might hope for.

Adjusting to communal living is a challenge, especially when you're used to your own space. Pedro's macho vibe and Mayte's watchful eyes make for an interesting mix. And let's not forget the cultural nuances, like the double doors for deliveries and the unique bathroom scheduling gymnastics.

Adam's school transition adds another layer to our adjustment. His initial struggles with the female teacher remind us of past challenges, but a change to a male teacher and a supportive learning environment turn his experience around.

As for me, the job hunt becomes a focal point. Apple's lengthy interview process tests my patience, and when that doesn't pan out, I broaden my search. My persistence pays off with an interview at a cybersecurity firm, even if the role isn't quite what I expected.

Through all these trials and tribulations, Cork begins to feel like home. The community's warmth, the blend of cultures in our shared house, and the small victories along the way weave together, creating a tapestry of our new life. It's a mix of chaos, learning, adapting, and finding joy in the unexpected — a true adventure in the Emerald Isle.

# Chapter 16
# Eire's Unexpected Twist of Fate

So there I was, on the relentless hunt for a job that didn't involve me saying, "Would you like a bag with that?" all day long. Pedro and Mayte, bless their hearts, couldn't wrap their heads around why I wasn't jumping at the chance to slap price tags on shelves. Pedro, the house-building hero, and Mayte, the childminder (currently on an indefinite break), just didn't get my master plan. "Listen, amigos," I'd tell them, "bagging a job at Ye Olde Shoppe isn't going to cut it when I'm eyeing a shiny desk in a swanky company."

Then, out of the blue, the universe threw me a bone. An interview invite landed in my inbox for a Sales Analyst position that sounded so much like my old gig at Diageo in Hungary, I had to double-check I wasn't being punked. Prepped and primed, I strutted into that interview like I owned the place, ready to sell them on the wonder that is moi.

The manager, a list-maker extraordinaire, grilled me with questions, jotting down my every word. I was in my element, recalling my glory days at IBM, Diageo, and Avis, where I was practically the office superhero. She was clearly impressed, and I could almost see the "Hired" stamp hovering above my head.

Next, I met with a dynamic duo from the team – a chatty chap and a bubbly lady. We hit it off, despite the guy's best efforts to throw me curveballs. I left the room buzzing, convinced the job was in the bag.

But wait, there's more! I had another interview lined up, this time for a customer service gig at the airport, which was about as appealing as a root canal. With Mayte's voice nagging in my head, I trudged to the interview, already mentally checked out and daydreaming about my earlier triumph.

Returning home, I found Mayte ready to dissect every aspect of my life, as per usual. Amidst our kitchen chitchat, I missed a call. It turned out to be the golden ticket – the big company wanted me, and they were ready to roll out the red carpet with a salary that made Amazon's offer look like pocket change.

I was ecstatic. No more language gymnastics –
my experience and English skills had sealed
the deal. I had proved to Pedro and Mayte
that I wasn't just chasing rainbows. With a
job that respected my weekends and bank
holidays, I was ready to soar. Eat your heart
out, job market – I'm the new queen in town!

# Chapter 17
# Glass Walls and Spanish Calls

So there I was, settled into my fancy new job, still green but nailing it. The office was a glass palace, folks – right next to city hall, no less. I mean, who needs walls when you can have panoramic views of the River Lee? Our desk spot wasn't exactly front-row to nature's spectacle, but the kitchen and meeting room? Chef's kiss! Picture this: an open-plan lounge meets a high-tech kitchen, all chic and shiny, where you could brew your coffee while eyeing the entire city center. Talk about a room with a view!

This place wasn't just a feast for the eyes; it was social central. The canteen was the hot spot, buzzing with chatter and the smell of freshly brewed coffee. I even buddied up with the cleaning lady and the building manager – the ultimate gossip duo. Not that I'm into the whole office drama scene, but a little tea-spilling never hurt, right?

One day, I heard about a Peruvian colleague on our floor. Eager for a dash of home, I zipped over and dropped a "Hola!" Her name? Geraldine. And through her, I met the coolest crew: Javier from cybersecurity (also our unofficial Spanish squad captain), Enrique from UI design, Gabriel and Pablo from Venezuela (also cybersecurity buffs), and a few others.

Despite our grand plans, our "Spanish-speaking club" never quite took off – except for this one epic pre-Christmas dinner meetup. Speaking of which, that Christmas party was the bomb! We hit the hotel bar, our little Spanish posse, and even Ana, our VP, let her hair down with us. She usually had this VP aura, but that night, she was one of the gang.

We didn't let the full tables at dinner dampen our spirits. We split up but stayed close, sharing laughs and stories. The party vibe was on point, especially when we hijacked the photo booth. Picture this: Ana squeezing in, Enrique half out of the frame – a hilarious mess. I ducked out at midnight with another non-drinker, leaving the rest to dance the night away.

In a nutshell, my job was ace, the office was a glass-cased dream, and I'd stumbled into the coolest, most unexpected Spanish-speaking club. Who knew a job could come with such perks? perks?

# Chapter 18
# License Quest and Cultural Fest

So, life with Adam was on the upswing - we had cash in our pockets and were living the dream in a fab city. However, our living situation was starting to feel like a cramped episode of a reality show.

Now, onto the epic saga of my driving license - or the lack thereof. Picture this: me, eager to hit the roads, but my instructor was more into the mommy life with her four little ones than teaching me the ways of the road. Just when I was about to get behind the wheel again, bam! Pregnancy and empty pockets threw a wrench in the works.

Enter Mayte with her "brilliant" suggestion: "Get your license in Spain, it's a piece of cake there!" Apparently, Irish driving tests are tougher than a steak at a cheap diner, or so she claimed. But here's a pro tip: taking advice from folks who haven't fully embraced the local vibes can lead to some wacky decisions. I mean, sure, it's comfy to stick with your own kind, but if you're not mingling with the locals, are you really getting the full experience?

I've always been a bit of a cultural chameleon. Spain felt like home, Hungary not so much, and now Ireland was starting to grow on me, with its laid-back, umbrella-ditching, sun-shy folks. And let's not even start on the differences in personal space and catcalling culture - let's just say, Irish road workers are gentlemen compared to their Hungarian counterparts.

Driven by Mayte's advice and my own adventurous spirit, I embarked on a license-getting odyssey that took me to the charming but remote Baza in Granada. The theory test there was tougher than a final boss in a video game, but I aced it with zero mistakes. Go me!

Navigating the maze of driving tests across Hungary, Spain, and Ireland was like comparing apples, oranges, and kiwis. In Hungary, it's a dance of theory, practice, and a splash of car mechanics. Spain's a bit more straightforward, but you're still doing the cha-cha with your instructor by your side. Ireland? Freedom! Pass your theory, grab a seasoned driver, and hit the road on your own terms.

So there I was, trying to master driving on the "wrong" side of the road, embracing my newfound Irish patience, and dodging raindrops without an umbrella. Life was an adventure, and I was riding shotgun, soon to be in the driver's seat.

# Chapter 19
# The Great Escape to Benalmádena

So, it was July, and I was buzzing with excitement for our upcoming getaway to Benalmádena. Adam and I were all set for a week of sun, sea, and sailing in a place that felt like our second home. Even though the rent for our holiday pad was sky-high compared to what we used to pay, we couldn't resist the call of our beloved Spanish haven.

Back in our current abode, life was turning into a soap opera. Our landlords, Mayte and Pedro, were sending us signals louder than a foghorn. Pedro, who fancied himself as the lord of the manor, was on a power trip that would make a telenovela villain blush.

Picture this: I'm in the kitchen, spreading some love by playing with one of the girls' hair, when Pedro suddenly appoints himself as the Hair Police, declaring, "Off-limits! Only I can touch her hair!" Uh, okay, Captain Creepy.

Then there was the Battle of the Thermostat. Our room was basically an icebox, and Pedro had a strict "no heating" policy after dark because, apparently, the upper floors turned into a sauna. So there I was, shivering in my socks, every time I dared to nudge the thermostat, Pedro would swoop in and dial it back to Antarctica.

One night, I tip-toed to the door, on a quest for a super important letter. Pedro must've thought I was plotting a heist because he came charging down, yelling like I'd just spray-painted the cat. The next morning, as Adam and I were heading out, we dared to use the main door. Pedro nearly had a meltdown. "That's not your door!" he barked. As if doors had VIP lists.

By this point, I was done. Ignoring Pedro became my new hobby, but he wasn't having any of it. His ego was bruised, and in his world, ignoring the alpha male was a cardinal sin.

Then, Mayte dropped the bombshell. It was time to pack our bags. Apparently, Pedro's comfort was the priority, and our main door escapades were the last straw. Their story about the sacred carpeted entrance was thinner than cheap toilet paper. But hey, any excuse in a storm, right?

So, after our sun-soaked week in Benalmádena, reality hit. We were on a mission to find a new nest in Cork, a city where finding a rental was like snagging a unicorn. But hey, on the bright side, at least we wouldn't have to deal with Pedro's domestic dictatorship anymore. Here's to new beginnings, sans the thermostat wars and door dramas!

# Chapter 20
# The Rental Rodeo and The
# Escape from Casa de Chaos

So there I was, embarking on the great Cork rental rodeo, where the ads were scarce, and the prices were sky-high. I was determined to find a new pad in our beloved neighborhood, but the rent was gobbling up half my salary. Talk about pricey!

Then, like a beacon of hope, a former colleague from IBM, who was way more into Facebook than I ever was, found a lead. A Hungarian couple had a room for rent. But after the whole living-with-others drama, I was craving some just-us space. Still, in the wild world of Cork rentals, beggars can't be choosers.

I dove into the rental viewing circus, where it was clear that unless you were a real estate agent's BFF, you were just part of the background crowd. I felt like an extra in a show where the main characters had already been cast.

Despite my reservations, I chatted with the Hungarian beach dwellers about their living room turned rental space. But, plot twist! They bailed, opting to help a buddy instead. Deep down, I was relieved. After the Mayte and Pedro show, sharing space was the last thing I wanted.

Then came another glimmer of hope: a room in the city center, a temporary setup with a

Hungarian family planning to return to Hungary. But the place was a no-go. It was as dark as a cave and as welcoming as a dentist's waiting room.

My rental hunt continued, leading me to an apartment that was a hard pass. It was tiny, moldy, and just plain sad. When I candidly shared my thoughts with the agent, he looked at me like I'd sprouted a second head. Direct feedback wasn't the Irish way, it seemed.

Phone calls were tricky with the Irish accent, so I played the email game, flaunting my salary and hoping for a bite. And then, a call came through mid-shower, a beacon of hope with a potential place in my preferred area. But when the promise fizzled out, I was back to square one.

Enter the grocery shop owners, local heroes who vouched for me to an auctioneer with a rental up for grabs. The place was a hidden gem, a ground-floor haven with its own garden, a rarity in the urban jungle.

I snagged the place, no fuss, no muss, just a handshake, a deposit, and a key. Adam and I were over the moon. He even got his own gaming room! And with the help of Jake, the grocery owner's son, we moved into our new abode, leaving the drama of Casa de Chaos behind.

Returning to tie up loose ends, I encountered Pedro, now playing the role of the concerned carpet inspector. I brushed off his accusations and made my exit, keys in hand and a sense of freedom in my heart.

Now, years later, passing by the old haunt doesn't sting as it used to. Life has moved on, and so have we. Mayte and Pedro are still tangled in their dance, but that's their rhythm to follow. As for me? I'm just grateful to be free from the whirlwind, living life on my terms, in a place we can truly call our own.

# Chapter 21
# Dutch Adventures and Hotel Escapades

So there we were, off to Amsterdam for a week because my new gig decided I needed to be a know-it-all, pronto. Adam and I landed in a 4-star hotel which, honestly, was more like 3.5 stars trying really hard. But hey, it was an upgrade from our usual hostel hopping.

The training was like a mini-United Nations gathering, but without the fancy earpieces. I was the token non-Dutch attendee, buddying up with a Polish gal while bonding over our mutual non-Dutchness. Meanwhile, Adam was living his best life, ordering room service like a young Rockefeller.

Our city escapades were a mixed bag. Dodging bikes and tourists felt like a live-action video game. But then we stumbled upon Ripley's Believe It or Not! museum, where we saw Michael Jackson immortalized in soda cans and the world's tallest man in a sitting position. You know, just your average Thursday.

Then there was the Body Worlds exhibit, which was like a biology lesson on steroids. Fascinating but slightly on the eerie side. And let's not forget our paddle boating saga – getting stuck under a bridge gave us a crash course in Dutch boating etiquette.

Next stop: Rotterdam, where the nhow hotel seriously made our Amsterdam digs look like a motel. The room was a glass palace with a shower that doubled as a panoramic window. Showering on the 14th floor with a view? Yes, please!

Adam was a fan of the buffet breakfast, turning into a mini-chef with his Nutella pancake concoctions. The view wasn't too shabby either, perched on the 7th floor with the city spread out below us.

Our little Rotterdam tour felt like we'd teleported to a Dutch Barcelona, minus the tapas. We even had a mini-Spanish reunion with the cleaning lady, bonding over the ex-pat life and government-enforced holiday savings. Who knew?

As all good things must end, we trammed our way back (sans ticket – rebel life) to catch our flight home. Amsterdam was a whirlwind of bikes, boats, and bizarre museums, while Rotterdam served up a slice of luxury life.

Back in Cork, I aced my test, armed with new knowledge and a bunch of quirky Dutch memories. And Adam? Well, he's probably still dreaming about those Nutella pancakes.

# Chapter 22
# The Spanish License Saga and Unplanned Adventures

Roll the drums, it was November, and the Spanish driving license mission was in its final act. After acing the theory in Baza and surviving a medical exam that felt more like a video game, it was time for the grand finale: the practical test. Carmen from the driving school was on the case, promising us a cozy spot in Baza for our grand driving adventure
.

Adam and I embarked on our journey from Cork to Málaga, then hopped on a bus to Granada, and another to Baza. Arriving with dreams of smooth driving lessons, we were greeted with a classic mix-up – no room, no plan, just us and our suitcases.

Carmen tried to patch things up by finding us an apartment that was more maze-like than homey. The place was tucked in a labyrinth of narrow alleys, giving off a strong 'hideout' vibe. The apartment was modest, with a kitchen that offered a view of the sky—if you craned your neck enough. The absence of windows in the bedroom was a downer, stirring up a mild case of claustrophobia in me.

A closer inspection revealed a less-than-sparkling interior. The previous tenants seemed to have vanished, leaving behind a mini-mess for us. Adam and I armed ourselves with cleaning supplies, declaring war on the grime. But doubts crept in. The bed—was it a haven for dust mites? My call to the landlord for fresh bedding was the final straw. Adam felt uneasy, and so did I. This wasn't the Spanish retreat we'd imagined. By evening, we bid adieu to the alley apartment, opting for a nearby hotel that, while cozy, threatened to drain our budget.

Thanks to a driving school owner with a heart, we landed in a pension that was more "Faulty Towers" than Ritz, run by a lovely Romanian family. Amidst this, I was zipping through Baza with a driving instructor who seemed more interested in her lunch dates than my driving skills. The driving lessons were a carousel of personalities, each taking their turn behind the wheel while I gleaned tips from the back seat. However, my lessons felt off-script compared to the others. The routes were different, and there was a nagging feeling that my fate was sealed before I even took the test. Spoiler alert: the test was a bust, pre-decided over tapas, no doubt.

As Adam turned our pension room into a gaming den, I mingled with other driving hopefuls, shared churros con chocolate, and soaked in the local hospitality. Our weekend detour to Benalmádena was a nostalgia trip, but our "hostel" turned out to be someone's spare room with a weird lady and a view of a wall. Classic Spain.

Back in Baza, the driving test drama unfolded as expected. With my bank account gasping for air, my guardian angel in Hungary swooped in to save our last supper in Spain. The pin code fiasco at the pension bar was just the cherry on top of our "stranded tourist" sundae.

Next up: Alicante, where our hostel hopes were dashed by a rave-like atmosphere unsuitable for a ten-year-old. With every accommodation door slamming shut, we finally found sanctuary thanks to a compassionate receptionist and my ever-patient Chinese colleague.

Our Alicante exploration was a mix of beach fun and McDonald's mishaps, with Adam turning into a little amusement park socialite. The journey back was a nail-biter, filled with financial gymnastics and more help from friends.

Landing back in Shannon, we navigated the final hurdle – a hotel mix-up that almost left us camping in the lobby. But Ireland smiled upon us, and we found solace in a cozy room and a hearty breakfast.

As Cork's familiar lights welcomed us home, Adam and I shared a sigh of relief. We were back in our haven, richer in stories and wiser in the unpredictable art of travel. This adventure was a crash course in resourcefulness, a reminder of the kindness of strangers, and a vow to never, ever, leave home without double-checking the pin code.

# Chapter 23
# Budapest Christmas and Office Shenanigans

Post our Spanish escapade, Adam and I opted for a low-key Christmas trip to Budapest to see my mom. Without a direct flight from Cork, we embarked on a mini-odyssey via Dublin, clocking in a solid three-hour bus trek to the airport. At least the universe threw us a bone with a direct flight back to Cork.

Our Budapest stay was a cozy affair at my mom's, sprinkled with a visit to Esmeralda and her beau, Manuel. Back at work, life was less about spreadsheets and more about navigating the peculiarities of my coworkers. Picture this: I'm sandwiched between Olivia, the noise detector, who could hear a pin drop a mile away, and Karen, who, bless her, had a personal vendetta against deodorant.

The guys on the other side of the office were living the dream—munching away, cracking jokes, basically embodying office goals. There I was, stuck in no-woman's land, day-dreaming about trading places with them. Olivia even had the Italian guy modding his fan to ninja levels of quiet because God forbid it disturbed her peace.

One day, with the office deserted for lunch, I dared to bring some french fries back to my desk. Cue Karen's unexpected entrance, and my snack time turned into a solo pity party on the back stairs. Why was enjoying some fries at my desk such a crime in an empty office?

Whenever the girl drama got too much, I'd seek refuge with Javier, my personal ray of Spanish sunshine. His laid-back attitude was my therapy: "Just chill, everything's cool." If only it were that simple. Karen wasn't thrilled about my growing rapport with my Chinese colleague, sparking a silent war where my fast learning became her kryptonite. She played the blame game like a pro, making sure our boss saw me as the error-prone newbie, despite my meticulous nature.

In a twist of fate, my venting sessions introduced me to Javier's manager, who became my unofficial career mentor. Diving into cybersecurity was my goal, and he was my guidebook, suggesting I get cozy with Python, hacking, and networking. An informal canteen chat later, and I was on the brink of joining his team—until 2020 decided to unleash its plot twist: COVID-19.

The pandemic slammed the brakes on my team transfer, with hiring freezes and remote work becoming the new normal. And to think, if we had stayed in Benalmádena, we'd be in the eye of the tourism storm. Instead, we were safely tucked away in Cork, riding out the global pause. In the grand scheme of things, munching 'chips' in isolation and dodging office politics seemed like child's play.

# Chapter 24
# The Lockdown Learning Spree
# and Certification Craze

Lockdown had us all cooped up, but not me —I was on a mission to cyber-upgrade myself. Thanks to Javier, my cyber-savvy amigo, I stumbled upon a couple of state-funded cybersecurity courses. A little admin hiccup later, and boom, I was double-booked: Networking at 6pm, Python programming at 7pm. Well, more like simultaneously, but who's counting?

The Python course was a bit of a head-scratcher. The instructor seemed to be winging it, leaving me more befuddled than enlightened. So, I'd have my Python class playing on one laptop while diving deep into the world of networking on another. My networking instructor was a cable wizard, showing off his latest tech toys like they were rare gems. I ended up learning Python in a virtual lab, teaching myself the ropes while the original class turned into background noise.

Lockdown life wasn't a huge shift for me. I'm a bit of a germaphobe at heart—always have been, pandemic or not. In Hungary, my homeland, if you so much as sanitize your hands, you get the side-eye, so I mastered the art of door-opening with my feet. And Blarney Castle's famous stone? No thank you, I'm not about to swap spit with a rock, no matter how lucky it's supposed to be.

Working from home was my little slice of heaven, no more tiptoeing around my peculiar colleagues. There was the noise-hater on one side, the smelly-snacker on the other, and here I was, stuck in the middle, dreaming of joining the boys' club on the other side of the office where eating at your desk wasn't a cardinal sin.

As the world turned virtual, I dove headfirst into my courses, nailing the Python test under my instructor's virtual watchful eye. Networking was next, with a twist of fate bringing me and Javier together at the instructor's house for our respective tests. Imagine that, a mini-reunion in the middle of an exam session!

Next up was the security course, a natural sequel to my networking saga. The instructor might not have been as passionate about firewalls as he was about fiber optics, but the knowledge was golden. And there I was, enrolling in yet another course, because why stop at one when you can juggle two?

The test days were a mix of excitement and nerves. For Python, I turned my living room into an exam hall. For networking, I hitched a ride with my buddy Sean, only to bump into Javier, making it feel like a cybersecurity study group rather than a solo mission.

Despite the hurdles—the online chaos, the overlapping schedules, the last-minute test location changes—I emerged victorious, certifications in hand. Five shiny badges of cyber honor, and even a bonus one for my driving theory test in Ireland, because why not add a bit of road knowledge to my growing collection of skills?

As for driving lessons, that had to wait. Ireland's rules meant a six-month gap between theory and practice. So there I was, a newly minted cyber whiz with a learner's permit, ready to conquer the digital and the asphalt jungles, just as soon as I found someone willing to ride shotgun with a newbie driver.

# Chapter 25
# Mallorca Misadventures and the Reunion

The heart of summer found me a tad blue, missing my feathery buddy, the robin who'd become a regular guest in my garden. My open-door policy had welcomed him for his favorite treats right inside my bedroom—those peanut butter suet pellets with mealworms were his jam! But my driving theory test turned my room into a no-fly zone for him, and just like that, my little friend took a sabbatical. Thankfully, he made a grand comeback a few months later, fluttering straight back to my hand as if he'd never left.

Out of the blue, my sister dangled the idea of a sunny getaway to Mallorca. She figured I was craving some vitamin sea, not knowing that Cork's beaches had done a fine job keeping my tan game strong. Yet, the thought of reconnecting with her and my nephew after ages was too good to pass up.

Upon landing, we were thrown a curveball—my sister was in the COVID club. There we were, in sunny Mallorca, navigating a maze of health protocols. Thankfully, Adam and I were in the clear. Turns out, my nephew was the unwitting trendsetter of the virus in their household. My sister, mistaking her symp-toms for a flu, was none the wiser until we rocked up.

Cabin crew life had its perks, but it also made my sister an easy target for the pesky virus.

Now grounded, she faced a mandatory timeout, turning our vacation into a bit of a staycation. Let's just say, cohabiting with my sister, who's not the easiest nut to crack, turned the heat up on family dynamics. The tension was real, folks.

Adam and I sought refuge in exploratory walks, scoping out the local scene, which, to be honest, wasn't the Mallorca you'd write home about. Just the beach and not much else. My sister, with her prickly persona, wasn't exactly Ms. Popular with the locals, adding another layer of spice to our island escapade.

But as the days rolled by, the ice thawed, and we even shared some good times, discovering a beach that was straight out of a travel brochure. My sister, a seasoned globe-trotter, might have seen it all, from Cancun's shores to the glaciers at the world's end, but for me, this was a slice of paradise.

Back in Cork, with barely time to unpack, we were gearing up for our next adventure to Budapest. Esmeralda, my BFF, was tying the knot with Manuel, and there was no way we'd miss it. Amidst the wedding buzz, my landlord decided to upgrade our domestic life with a swanky new digital washing machine. Because why not add a bit of home appliance excitement to our whirlwind summer?

# Chapter 26
# The Wedding Whirlwind and Homemade Treasures

Before jet-setting to Mallorca, I was deep in my craft cave, concocting some heartfelt gifts for Esmeralda's wedding. Picture this: a flamenco dancer couple, etched into a mirror, a scene so Spanish it could dance off the glass. Then there was the card, not your run-of-the-mill congratulations, but a mini art piece with Esmeralda and Manuel's faces, dressed in cloth-cut couture. They were over the moon with it, and that mirror? Now it's a wall celebrity in their home.

But wait, there's more. I went tech-meets-tradition with an external hard drive, a treasure chest of Spanish cinematic gems, topped off with a paper flamenco fan, because why not? Our shopping spree in Mallorca's Chinese bazaars paid off when we found the perfect flamenco-dancer cushion cover—talk about serendipity!

Fast forward to Budapest, where the wedding magic unfolded. We hopped on a bus filled with chatter and excitement, diving headfirst into a sea of Spanish warmth and hospitality.

The wedding was a tear-jerker, a true love fest that had even my usually stoic self reaching for the tissues. The feast was a culinary delight, and our table mates, Manuel's cousins, were the life of the party, ensuring laughs were in no short supply.

Post-feast, the fun escalated with games and dancing. Adam and I, however, hit a bit of a snag—tummy troubles and a dash of breathlessness thanks to our shared intolerance to alcohol and histamine. Just when we thought our party was over, Esmeralda's mom and her partner came to our rescue, whisking us away in a taxi.

The wedding was a burst of joy, a vibrant mix of love, laughter, and a touch of Spanish flair. Even now, it's a fond memory that brings smiles and a reminder of the infectious spirit of Spanish fiestas.

# Chapter 27
# School Bells and Cyber Spells

So, here's the scoop: Adam trotted off to secondary school, and boy, was he pumped! Unlike most kiddos here in Ireland who start primary at the tender age of four and then hit secondary after the 6th year, Adam's a bit of a school-hopping pro. With a history of changing schools faster than I change my Netflix preferences, he was more than ready for this new adventure.

Now, let's gab about my job saga. After pouring my heart into my work and even acing my cybersecurity studies, my performance review was as disappointing as finding out your favorite series got canceled.

Apparently, not being keen on hosting governance calls was a bigger deal than I thought. Talk about a plot twist!

But hey, every cloud has a silver lining, right? My manager hinted at other opportunities, nudging me towards a role in vulnerability management. Not exactly the cyber dream I had in mind, but it was a step in the right direction.

Meanwhile, my buddy Javier dropped a juicy tidbit: his team was almost a ghost town post-lockdown! With the team's scope shifting faster than Irish weather, I saw my chance and shot an email to his new manager, pitching myself for a junior cybersecurity role.

Fast forward to the interview - it was more like a friendly chat than a grilling session. The team seemed cool, and I was all in for joining the cyber squad. After a nerve-wracking wait and some corporate red tape, I got the offer – and it came with a salary bump that had me doing a happy dance!

While all this job excitement was unfolding, I was on a mission to transform my garden into a tropical paradise. From a sad patch of weeds to a lush, plant-filled haven, I was channeling my inner gardener like there's no tomorrow. I even embarked on a "Save the Lawn" operation to fend off those pesky cats marking their territory all over my green masterpiece.

And let's not forget my feathered and furry garden visitors – from my dear departed robin buddy to the magpie pals and those sneaky feline intruders. It's like a wildlife soap opera out here!

So there you have it – Adam's acing his school game, I've landed my dream cyber gig, and my garden's turning into the set of "Jumanji." Life's a wild ride, and I'm here for it, ready to tackle whatever comes next with a smile and a bit of that Irish luck.

Hey there! I'm Timea M Kiraly, rocking the solo mom gig by choice. Born under the Mexican sun thanks to my diplomat dad, I grew up with a suitcase in one hand and a map in the other. Madrid was my playground, but Hungary? Not so much my jam. I always had my heart set on Spain, but life, that cheeky little thing, had other plans.

So, here I am, living the dream (for real!) in a spot that's like a postcard come to life. Think stunning beaches, ocean breezes, and a bunch of folks who are as chill as a Netflix binge session. I wanted a life where my kiddo and I could thrive without the constant juggle of making ends meet, and voila— mission accomplished.

Join me on this wild ride where I've swapped paprika for the salty sea air, proving that dreams do come true, with a bit of grit, a dash of grace, and a whole lot of motherly love.